# The Display
# TOILET
## Disaster!

### Marcy Schaaf

In The Display Toilet Disaster!,
a simple trip to the hardware store turns into a day
no one will forget! When a boy sees something that
looks like the perfect bathroom solution, he makes a
big mistake that leaves his Aunt Claire racing to stop
him.
This funny and unexpected adventure will remind
readers that not everything in a store is what it seems
—especially toilets on display! Get ready for laughs,
surprises, and a lot of fun!

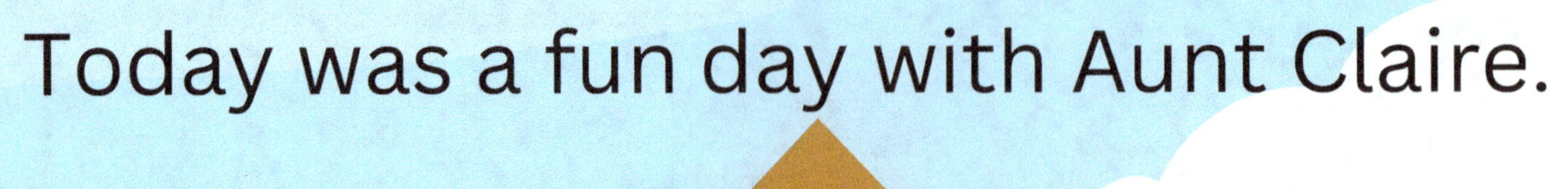

Today was a fun day with Aunt Claire.

We went to the hardware store
so much to share!

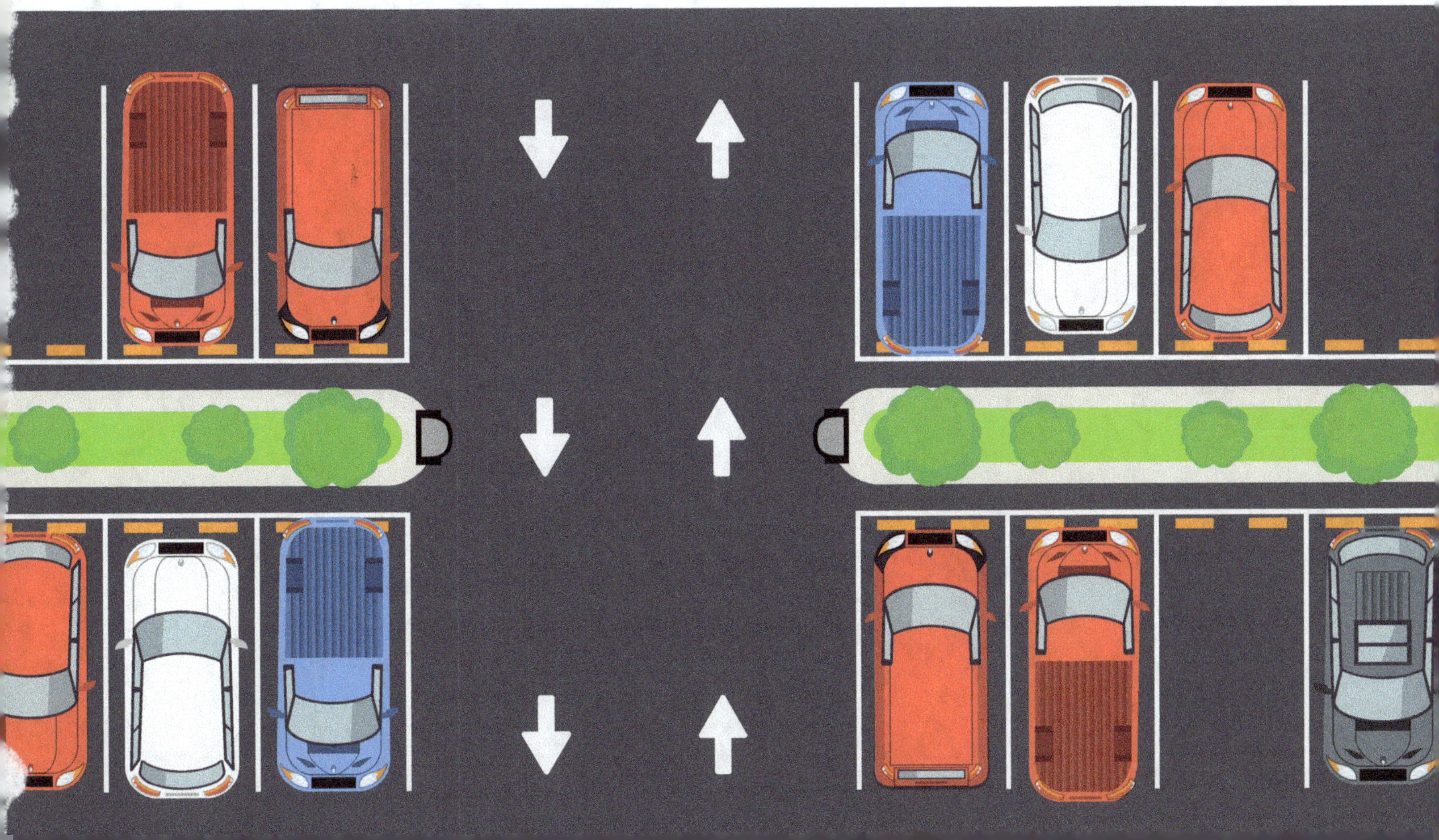

We looked at tools, paint, and brushes too.

But then I said, "Aunt Claire, I need to poo!"

She nodded and said, "Let's go to
the back,"

The public restroom was on the right track.

But on the way something caught my eye!

A row of display
toilets shiny and
high!

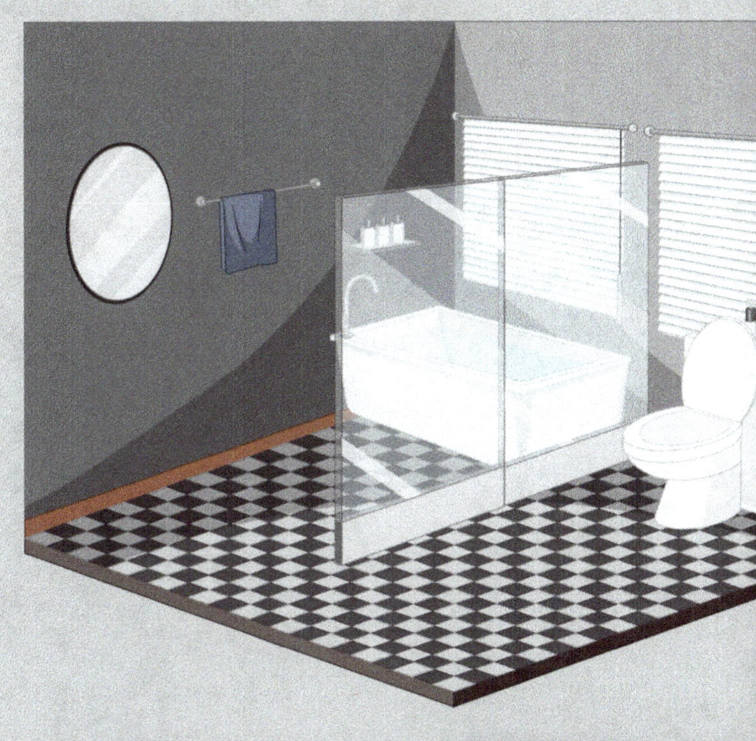

I pulled down my pants and sat down with glee!

# Before Aunt Claire could even stop me!

She ran fast waving her arms in the air!

"No, not that toilet! That's not fair!"

I smiled and sighed feeling just right.

But Aunt Claire's face was a terrible sight!

"It's a display!
You can't do that here!"

Her voice shook with a little fear.

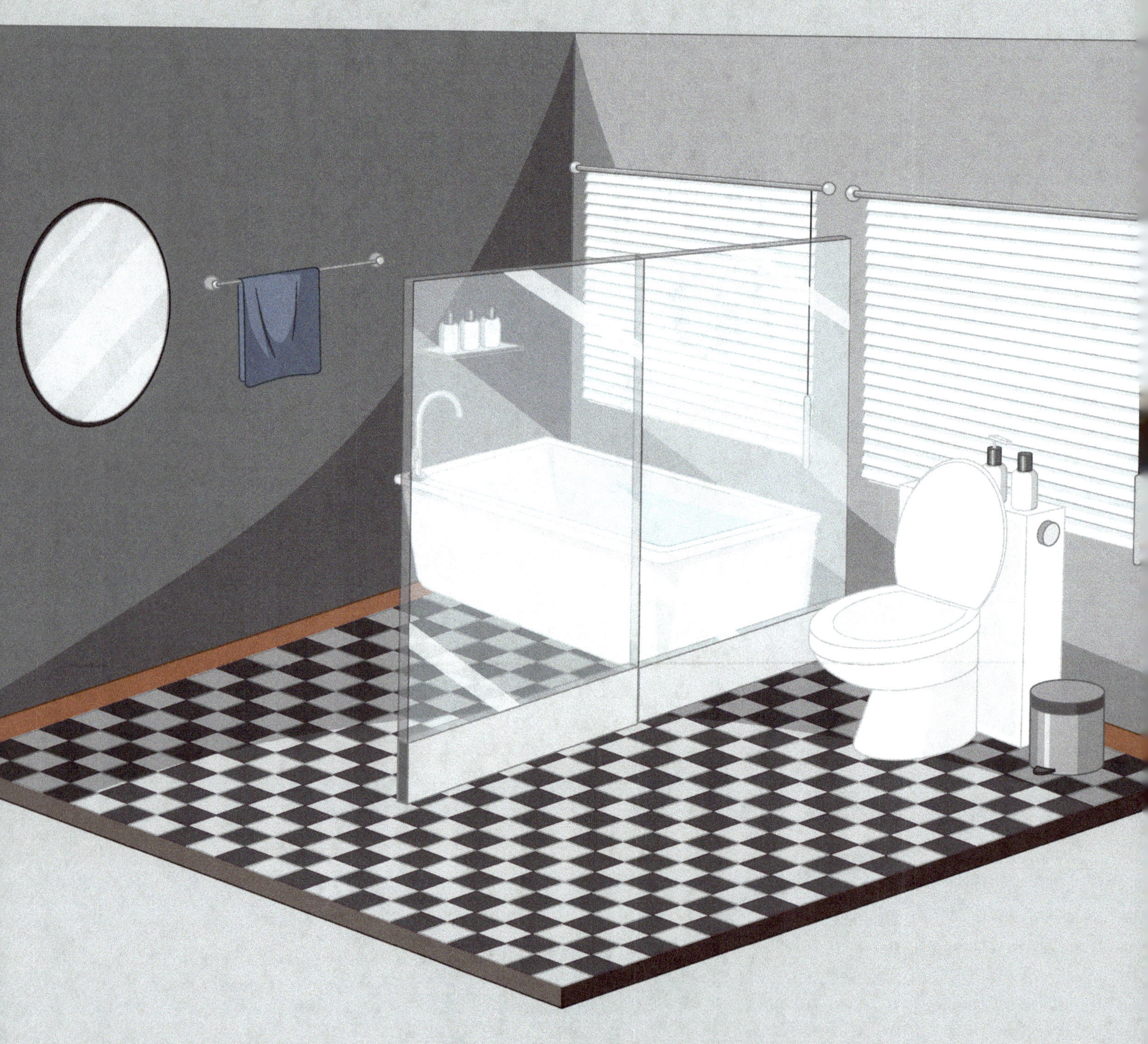

I stood up quick, confused and slow...

"Why not? It's a toilet, though!"

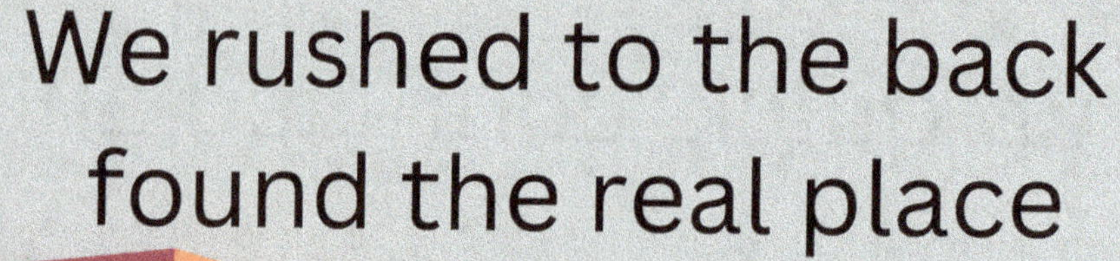

We rushed to the back
found the real place

Aunt Claire wiped sweat from
her worried face.

The store clerk saw
and gave us a smile

But Aunt Claire frowned for quite a while.

We cleaned up fast
and walked to the door.

# I learned:
## toilets in stores are just for décor!

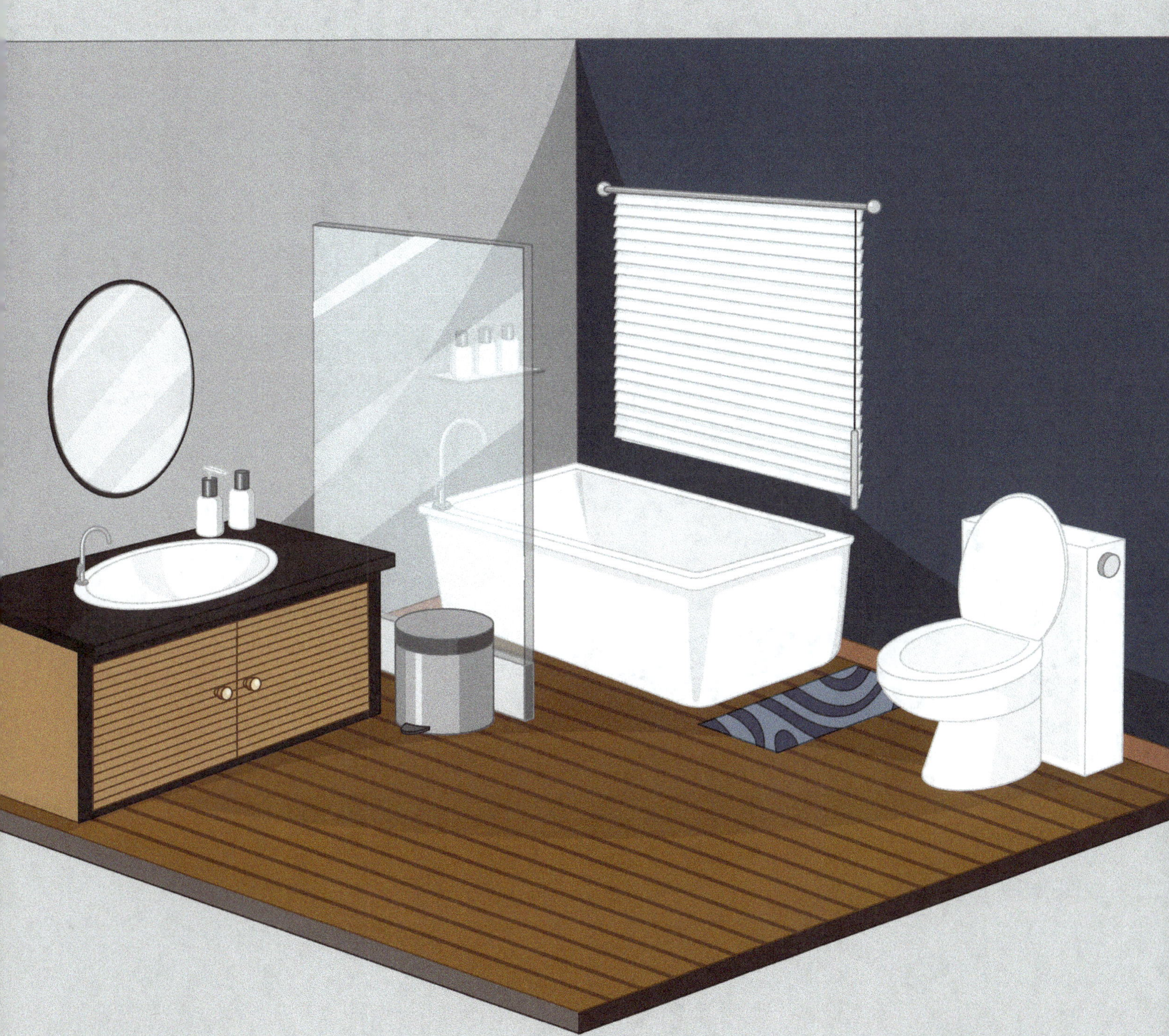

Now I know, next time we go,
ask before using anything on show!

Aunt Claire laughed when
we got outside!

But I felt a little bit shy inside.

We giggled all the way back home

With stories to share wherever we
roam!

# The End

# Books By Schaaf

www.BookBySchaaf.com

Find us at: